LIGHTNING BOLT BOOKS™

Meet a Baby Zebra

Lisa Owings

Lerner Publications
Minneapolis

Content Consultant: Dr. Mark C. Andersen, Department of Fish Wildlife and Conservation Ecology, New Mexico State University

Lerner Publications Company
A division of Lerner Publishing Group, Inc.
241 First Avenue North
Minneapolis, MN 55401 USA

For reading levels and more information, look up this title at www.lernerbooks.com.

Library of Congress Cataloging-in-Publication Data

Owings, Lisa.
    Meet a baby zebra / Lisa Owings.
        pages cm. — (Lightning bolt books. Baby African animals)
    Includes index.
        ISBN 978-1-4677-8114-5 (lb : alk. paper) — ISBN 978-1-4677-8371-2 (pb : alk. paper) —
    ISBN 978-1-4677-8372-9 (eb pdf)
        1. Zebras—Infancy—Juvenile literature. I. Title.
    QL737.U62O95 2015
    599.665'71392—dc23   2014044200

Manufactured in the United States of America
1 – BP – 7/15/15

Table of Contents

Born to Run

Did you see that blurry bundle of stripes? Baby zebras are on the move soon after birth. They have to keep up with their family group. One male zebra protects many mothers and young.

A herd of zebras runs across the African plains.

A zebra grows in its mother's belly for about one year. Then she is ready to give birth.

A mother zebra gives birth alone.

Foals can walk and run within one hour of being born.

Zebra foals are born feetfirst. They flop onto the ground. Their mother licks them clean. Foals try to stand right away. They take their first steps on wobbly legs.

6

Newborn zebras weigh around 70 pounds (32 kilograms). That is about as much as a large dog. Adult zebras can weigh as much as four refrigerators, or up to 850 pounds (385 kg)!

Baby zebras grow very quickly.

Zebra foals have fuzzier coats than their parents. Each zebra has its own stripe pattern. Can you tell them apart?

Foals' stripes are often brown instead of black.

Mothers and newborn zebras take time to bond. Then they return to the group.

Alone time is important for a mother and her foal.

Life on the Plains

Baby zebras have to learn quickly to survive in the wild. They mainly learn from their mothers.

Male zebras stay busy watching over the group.

Foals nurse when they get hungry. Their mothers teach them which grasses to eat.

Zebra foals follow their mothers as they graze.

Zebra foals can gain up to 1 pound (0.5 kg) each day! That is as much as four sticks of butter.

Baby zebras soon grow into their long legs.

Other hungry animals roam the plains too. Foals must learn to avoid hyenas and lions. Foals also must stay away from leopards and cheetahs.

Lions are one predator zebras must try to escape.

Zebras can run fast when they need to.

Zebras form circles around the young to protect them. The adults kick and bite to fight off predators.

Mothers groom their babies to keep them clean. Grooming also helps them bond. At night, baby zebras sleep while parents stand watch.

Zebra mothers teach foals how to groom one another.

Where the Grass Is Greener

Baby zebras drink only their mothers' milk for the first week. Then they begin eating grasses and other plants. But foals still drink milk from their mothers too.

Foals stop nursing between seven and eleven months.

When foals grow older and stop nursing, they must get all of their nutrients from plants. It isn't always easy.

Zebras eat mainly dry grasses and bushes.

Some zebras stay in one place to graze and rest.

Some young zebras live in areas with plenty of food year-round. But others live in areas where there is only enough food for part of the year. They must migrate during the dry season.

When zebras migrate, small groups come together to form large herds. The herds travel for hundreds of miles. They look for water and fresh grasses.

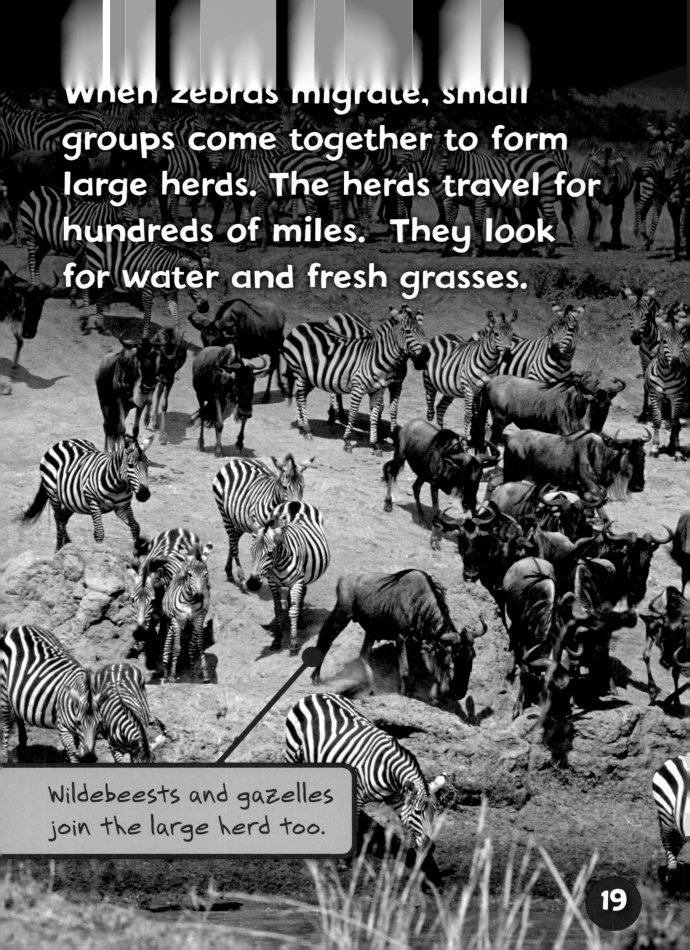

Wildebeests and gazelles join the large herd too.

Starting New Families

Young zebras do not stay with their parents forever. They leave the group when they are one to three years old.

Young zebras go out on their own before starting a family.

Females choose a mate and join his new family group. They often start having babies around age three.

Most females have one foal every two years.

Males form groups with other males. They practice fighting.

Males fight one another to create new families.

Later, the males will battle over females. Each male will try to start his own family group.

Zebras drink water at least once a day.

Most of an adult zebra's day is spent eating. Zebras have to eat lots of plants to stay healthy.

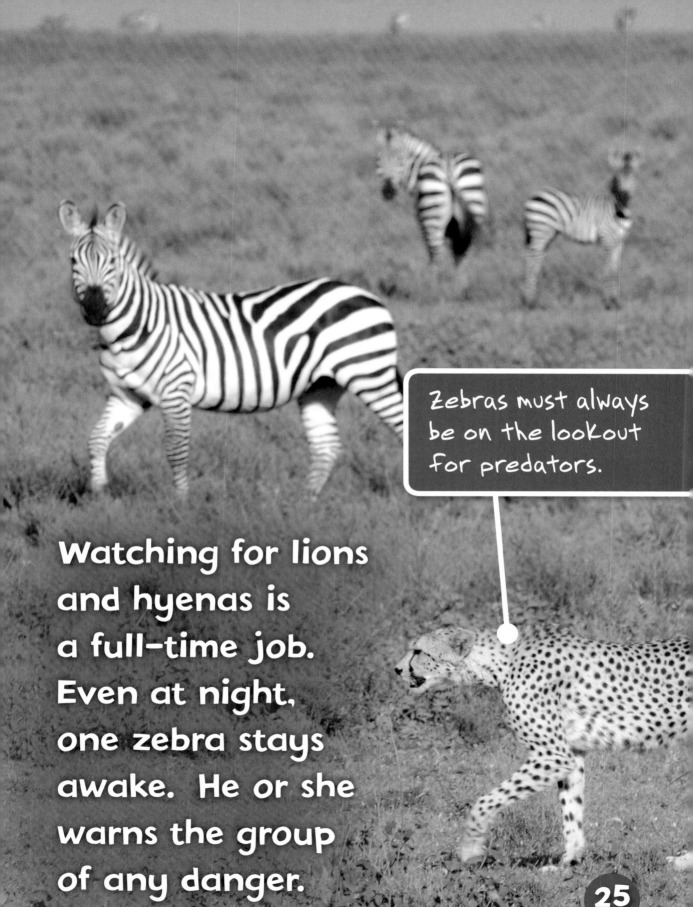

Zebras must always be on the lookout for predators.

Watching for lions and hyenas is a full-time job. Even at night, one zebra stays awake. He or she warns the group of any danger.

Once they have left their mothers, female zebras stay with the same group their whole adult lives. Males may leave their group for a new one.

Zebras live for around twenty years in the wild. They spend their lives as part of the group. But they are each as unique as their stripes!

Zebra Life Cycle

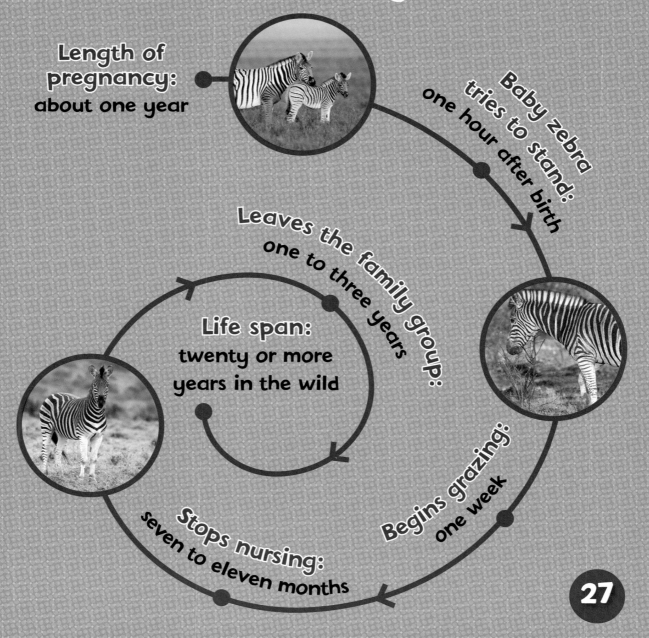

Length of pregnancy: about one year

Baby zebra tries to stand: one hour after birth

Leaves the family group: one to three years

Life span: twenty or more years in the wild

Begins grazing: one week

Stops nursing: seven to eleven months

Habitat in Focus

- Zebras live in grasslands in southern and eastern Africa.

- Zebras need plenty of grass for grazing. They also stay close to water. Zebras may travel for hundreds of miles to find food and water.

- People sometimes take over the land and water that zebras need. But zebras living in the plains are still doing well in the wild.

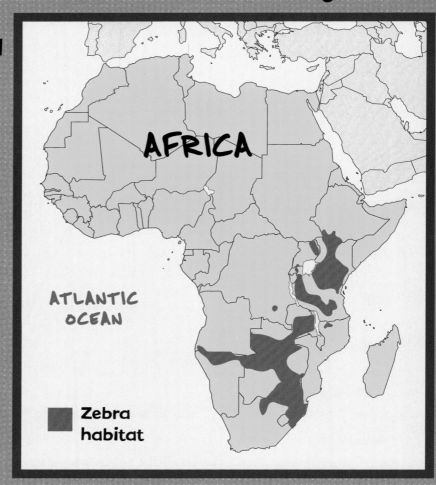

AFRICA

ATLANTIC OCEAN

Zebra habitat

Fun Facts

- A zebra's teeth never stop growing. Chewing grasses wears the teeth down.

- Zebras often sleep standing up. This lets them quickly escape danger at night.

- Some zebras are black with white stripes. Others are mostly dark. Many plains zebras have lighter stripes between black ones.

- Zebras love to chat! They make loud cries or barks and soft snorts.

Glossary

foal: a baby zebra

groom: to clean and care for

herd: a group of animals that lives together

migrate: to move to different areas at certain times of the year

nurse: to drink milk from the mother

nutrient: a substance that animals, people, and plants need to live and grow

plain: a large, flat grassland

predator: an animal that hunts and kills other animals for food

Further Reading

Anderson, Sheila. *What Can Live in a Grassland?* Minneapolis: Lerner Publications, 2011.

Latham, Irene. *Dear Wandering Wildebeest: And Other Poems from the Water Hole.* Minneapolis: Millbrook Press, 2014.

National Geographic Kids: Zebra
http://kids.nationalgeographic.com/animals/zebra

Raatma, Lucia. *Plains Zebras.* New York: Children's Press, 2014.

San Diego Zoo Kids: Zebra
http://kids.sandiegozoo.org/animals/mammals/zebra

Zobel, Derek. *Zebras.* Minneapolis: Bellwether Media, 2011.

Index

Photo Acknowledgments

The images in this book are used with the permission of: © Chris Kruger SA/iStock/Thinkstock, pp. 2, 8; © Mattia ATH/Shutterstock Images, pp. 4, 14; © AfriPics/Alamy, p. 5; © Mark Levy/Alamy, p. 6; © Gerrit de Vries/iStock/Thinkstock, p. 7; © EcoPrint/Shutterstock Images, pp. 9, 22, 24, 27 (top), 31; © TanzanianImages/iStock/Thinkstock, pp. 10, 17, 27 (bottom right); © Steffen Foerster/Shutterstock Images, p. 11; © Palenque/iStock/Thinkstock, p. 12; © Mogens Trolle/Shutterstock Images, p. 13; © Vadim Petrakov/Shutterstock Images, p. 15; © Nico Smit/iStock/Thinkstock, p. 16; © Humpata/iStock/Thinkstock, p. 18; © Anup Shah/Digital Vision/Thinkstock, p. 19; © FourOaks/iStock/Thinkstock, pp. 20, 27 (bottom left); © ottoduplessis/iStock/Thinkstock, p. 21; © Ingram Publishing/Thinkstock, p. 23; © Laura Romin and Larry Dalton/Alamy, p. 25; © Philip de Villiers Steyn/iStock/Thinkstock, p. 26; Red Line Editorial, p. 28; © prapass/Shutterstock Images, p. 30.

Front cover: © Hoberman Collection/Universal Images Group/Getty Images

Main body text set in Johann light 30/36.

THE ENDURING COSMOS

To one who looks at a single leaf · ·
　　　　and sees the essence of life

　　— and finds the infallible rhythms
　　　　of the stars and tides · · ·
　　　　　　· · the earth and the sun
　　reflected in every tree that grows · · · · · · ·

BLOCK-PRINTS and WORDS by GWEN FROSTIC

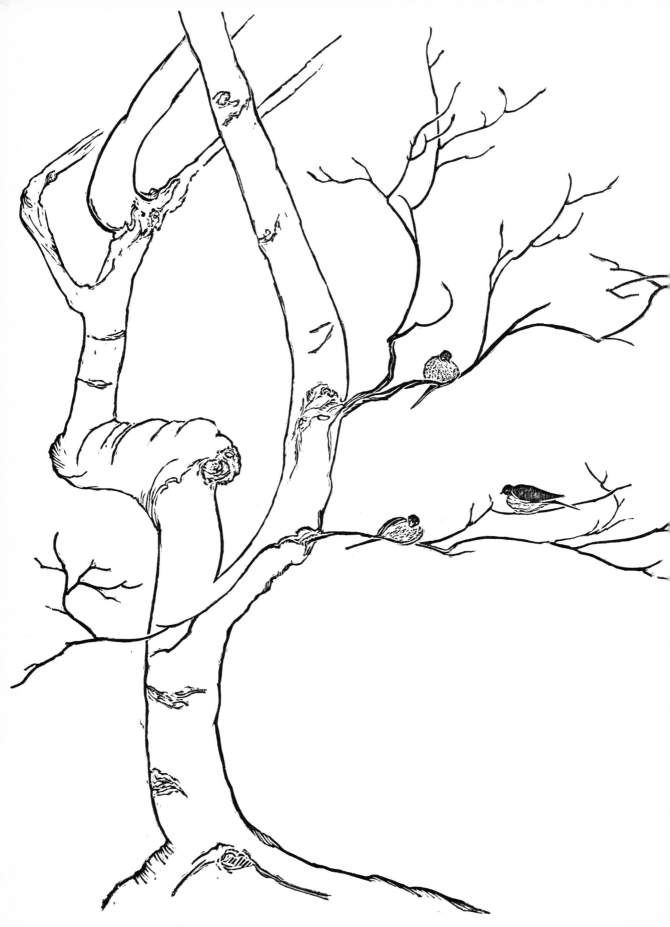

Shrouded in mystery -

         - - amorphous in concept

               - - - the future . . . .

- - yet -
the source of all the energy of earth shines on - - -
    the moving force that shaped all things
        ever since the primal dawn — shall not waver . . . .

Day will follow each night that comes —
        winter will pass - - - springs awaken . . . .

    Man and nature will be one
            - - - as they have always been - -
    interlocked interminably with the rhythms of the universe . . . . .

    There is assurance in recurring patterns - -
      in all the diversities and transformations -
        — the drama of evolution
            will never cease . . . . . .

    Birds will sing their ancient songs - -
        fresh winds will blow across the land . .

Man will feel the pulse of universal life - - -

      — — — and know its poignant loveliness . . . . . .

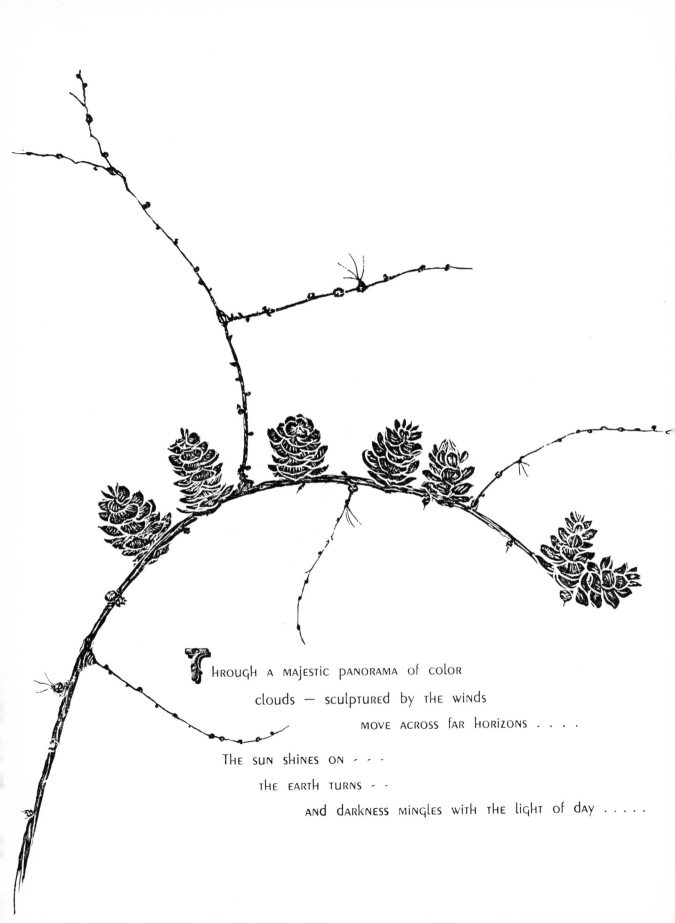

Through a majestic panorama of color
    clouds — sculptured by the winds
            move across far horizons . . . .

The sun shines on - - -
    the earth turns - -
            and darkness mingles with the light of day . . . . .

Gulls soaring above the lake - -
        and tall grasses waving on the sands
                    are silhouetted by the radiance . . . . .

The wings of moths begin to flutter - -
            the life of night is stirring
                in the meadows - - the ponds -
                    - across the mystic dunes - - -
            in the solitudes of the woods
                        - - - and swamplands - -
        each following an inherent rhythm of its own
                    — as those of the day follow theirs —

        attuned to the great synchronous rhythms
            that make up the universe -
                    - - - and will endure forever . . . .

Rhythms that cause the tides to rise - -
            produce night and day - - -
                mountains and running brooks -
                        spider webs and dew —
        determine what life shall live - -
                    - - - and where . . . .

Rhythms that sustain the equilibrium of the universe —
        the cyclical phenomena — and the continual melding of life - -
            create the harmonious unity and beauty
                                                of the entirety . . . . .

Old as time - - - -
                continuous as life - - - - -
                        the dominant influence in the universe . . . . .

    There is not a leaf upon a tree - -
                    no blade of grass - -
                                        or drop of dew - - -
            that escapes the reign of the rhythms . . . . .

All the life rhythms of
        the insects - birds - - flowers - - -
                        animals and human beings —
                concur to celebrate one great symphony . . . .

    A symphony man cannot direct - - - -
                                and should not try . . . . . .

    Born with great powers - - -
                        equalized by powerlessness
            man cannot beat his separate drums - - - -
                                nor go his way unheeding -
                for he is an inseparable part of the universe —
                    - - its grasses and trees -
                                the wind and the wings . . . . .

The mystery of the rhythms —

    - - is so simple - - - and so inevitable - - - -

                it defies elucidation - - -

    — yet - man will find assurance

          in the rising of the moon -

      - the budding of the willows

           as growth begins anew - - -

       the preciseness of each dawn - - - - -

      and comprehend the secret

         that guides his destiny . . . .

The secret that makes the wild bird

        fly uncharted skies - - -

         - sing - and build its nest

            each spring . . . .

The secret

    of multitudinous individual lives

      - with all their disasters and triumphs - -

        - - restless growth and realizations - - -

     melding with the majestic universal rhythms - - -

   from which emerges

      the awesome grandeur

        of everlasting life . . . .

Rhythmic equilibrium — —

      - - powerful influences that assure the ratio
         of the air to the waters - - -
             - of all things to all things - -
      generates harmonious order within the universe . . . .

Never by caprice —
         but by design and order
                that defy man-made conceptions . . . .

Sometimes through total calamity —
    - - storms - - floods
           - quakes - and droughts
      — things that seem destructive
          in the eyes of man
             are vital
                to universal equalization. . . . .

And — by day-to-day use of individual lives - - -
                picked seemingly at random . . .

The development of each life on earth is keyed to its survival . .
  Each —
     an individual - for individualism is inherent to life itself -
      will protect itself - - and its right to be . . . . . .

  But balance must be served - - -
        life is the one source of life on earth - -
    always —
     lives are ending - - and lives are beginning
          as life goes on forever . . . .

In this complicated — yet extremely simple process
           of checks and balances
  no one thing will ever dominate the earth - - -
     for as the number of one species increases —
        the things it lives upon diminish - -
  - its food and shelter —
     the soil and the water — —
        until - it too - begins to ebb . . . .

Continuous natural symmetrization —
             of all the elements - -
                      insects - animals -
                            plants and humans - -
       is assurance of total diversity - endless beauty and harmony
                                 in this perpetual order . .

Unpredictable fluctuations -
             - variable tolerances - -
                      periods of acceleration - - -
             seem to challenge the premise of balance
         yet — as time reveals the entirety
                            balance remains infallible . . . .

The mind of man has the ability - -
                      if his emotions will let it - - -
             to work with balance and prevent man's
                            total catastrophe . . . .

Man can - by his own choice -
                 control his numbers -
                 curb his wanton waste
                      of materials and energy - -
             his destruction of the land
                 upon which he lives
                      - the air - - and the waters . . . .

Man must reverse his compulsion
                to balance life according to his
                                own desires . . . .

He must use with extreme caution
                the resources earth has accumulated
                                over millions of years - -
        conserve all forms of energy -
                aware that these things
                                are not his to extort . . . . . .

        A great revolution in the mind of man
                will create an understanding
                        of the absolute power
                                of natural equalization - - -

        an understanding that will lead to
                a world of harmony - beauty and peace -
                        without waste - - -
                                and without want . . . .

                It can — —
                        - - if man will . . . . . .

irds - insects - and tiny snails - -
                    grasses - mushrooms - - and flowers - - -
                            trees - animals - - and human beings —
        perpetual synthesis - - -
                    nature in rotation - - -
                            is forever generating new life . . . .

As each life receives other life unto itself —
                            - and is consumed by others
                    universal life - with all its immense beauty -
                                    is evolving . . . .

A mushroom growing on an old log in the woods
                            is gaining its life from a tree —
            in turn - will be transmuted to life in a snail
                            - - and a bird beyond - - -
            as the living force that once was a tree
                    goes through a milliard changes - - - -
                                never to be a tree again —
            - yet - life remains uninterruptable - - -
                    - an invisible chain that will not break . . . .

Life - not a thing complete unto itself — is an eternal process
                            of becoming - - - ever becoming . . . .

Never again will the exact combination of living cells
                            gather into one being —
        that is the essence of individualism - - - -
            the uniqueness of many segments blending together —
                        multitudes of cells forever changing . . . .

- generating universal orderliness - -
continuity - - - beauty —
and serenity . . . .

Reverberating in the human heart - - - assurance . . . . .
This day will come - and go - - - and come again . . . .

One that translates - - with deep sensitivity - - -
the message of the cycles —
will face each day with confidence -
fortitude that will calm the fears of man - - -
- the uncertainties that emerge from man's self-centeredness - -

His loss of the rapture
of commonplace occurrences
— the fascination of each
sunrise - - - -

and the evening star
as it follows its own
particular path . . . .

The verity of
everlasting harmony - -
is universal . . . .

Winter melts into spring - - time of miraculous suspense -
　　　spring bursts into summer with the elation of fulfillment - -
　　　　　　and ripens into the blazing colors of autumn - - -
　　　　　and - the exquisite loveliness of winter begins anew . . . .

And all the time the earth is turning - - -
　　　　　　　　　　　　　　　　ever turning - - -
　　　the silent moon is going around the earth - -
　　　　　　　　　　　the earth encircles the sun - -
　　　　　as all the stars follow their own recurring cycles . . . .

Winds rise and fall - -
　　　　great tides ebb and flow - - - -
　　　　　　cycles - - - within cycles - - -
　　　　　　　　　rhythmic successions —
　　　　the harmonious pattern that underlies all creation - -
　　　　　　　　- continuous as creation itself . . . . .

A cool breeze
　　meets a cloud in the sky above - -
　　　　— rains fall to the earth - - -
　　　　　　　to the brooks and the rivers
　　　　　　　　　　that run to the sea - - -
　　　　　　　　　the fountainhead of clouds . . . .
　　　　A recurrence complete unto itself . . . . .

From the fertile earth a great tree rises - -
　　　　　　　- a tree whose cycle spans many springs —
　　　in its leaves - tiny insects
　　　　　　　　that have but hours to live - -
　　　follow the invariable sequence of
　　　　　　birth - growth - - and death
　　　　　　　　shared by every living thing . . . . . .

THE SEQUENCE IS CONSTANT
— ONLY THE TIMING VARIES . . . .

ALL THE WINGS - - - AND ALL THE LEAVES —
EACH CREATURE OF THIS EARTH
THE ROCKS - THE WAVES - -
THE DUNES AND STARS
PURSUE A REGULAR INEVITABLE TEMPO —
THE INTRINSICALITY OF UNIVERSAL ORDER . . . . .

ALL THE NATURAL FUNCTIONS OF EACH LIFE -
THE SIMPLE ACTS OF EATING AND SLEEPING — —
- RECURRING ACTIVITIES CREATE THE
INHERENT CYCLE OF EACH LIFE . . . . . .

A CONSTANT SUCCESSION OF INCIDENTS
FUSE WITH EVER WIDENING CYCLES —
MERGE WITH UNIVERSAL OCCURRENCES -
DAYS AND NIGHTS -
THE SEASONS - -
YEARS - - - AND EONS . . . . .

MANIFESTATION OF THE MIRACULOUS COSMOS . . . .

THERE ARE FLOWERS THAT OPEN ONLY TO THE MORNING LIGHT
- OTHERS AS THE SUN REACHES ITS APEX
- AND SOME IN THE DARKNESS OF NIGHT - -

EACH — WITH AN INTRANSIGENT ORDER —
DISTINCTLY ITS OWN . . . .

The revolving periods in the lives
            of the birds - - and the insects - - -
                    coincide with those of the flowers —
                            as the cycles interweave . . . . .
        The call of the whip-poor-will is heard at twilight - -
            - - the owl flies silently through the darkness - - -
                - - - moths by night - - -
                        - - butterflies by the light of the sun . . . . . .

Individual cycles - -
            among a milliard others —
                within greater cycles - - -
                        - - - each functioning unto itself . . . .

Within this wondrous order
            nothing recurs precisely - - -
                each day is a little different —
                    springs may be warmer -
                        - - - or cooler - -
        but the succession of the seasons remains constant . . . .

    Birds return - nest - moult and grow new feathers - -
        the sap in the trees flows - buds open —
            leaves mature and fall - as always - - -
            and - in the ponds - spring peepers sing their songs -
                    - - pristine melodies - - forever new . . .

— now and then
            at fixed intervals - -
                there is a converging of cycles —
            creating extraordinary phenomena - -
                    the eclipse of the moon - - and the sun
                        — periods of lush growth
                            and times of great storms - - - -
        still the ancient rhythms beat on - - - in regular sequence   —

In all this synthesizing of living cells -

        throughout the merging and fusing of lives - -

                - the perpetual mutation —

    with all the diversity of shapes - forms and colors - -

           each species remains distinguishable - -

      for each passes on to its embryo

              that which it inherited . . . .

Although every seed may not develop

          into a great tree - - -

           nor each egg produce a tiny bird - -

     the living substance in these things is used over and over -

        never to be destroyed —

           and never wasted . . . .

In man's grasping toward his own economic security - - -

          - his obsession with his own comfort —

      he has ignored the natural process

            of continuous life . . . .

By seeing life only in small segments - -

        unmindful of the unity of the total universe

     he has havocked the delicate balance of the supreme order . . . . .

All of man's knowledge - -

        and all of man's skills —

            cannot create life . . . . .

Rhythmic equilibrium and the endless synthesis process

        are components in the never revealing entirety . . . . .

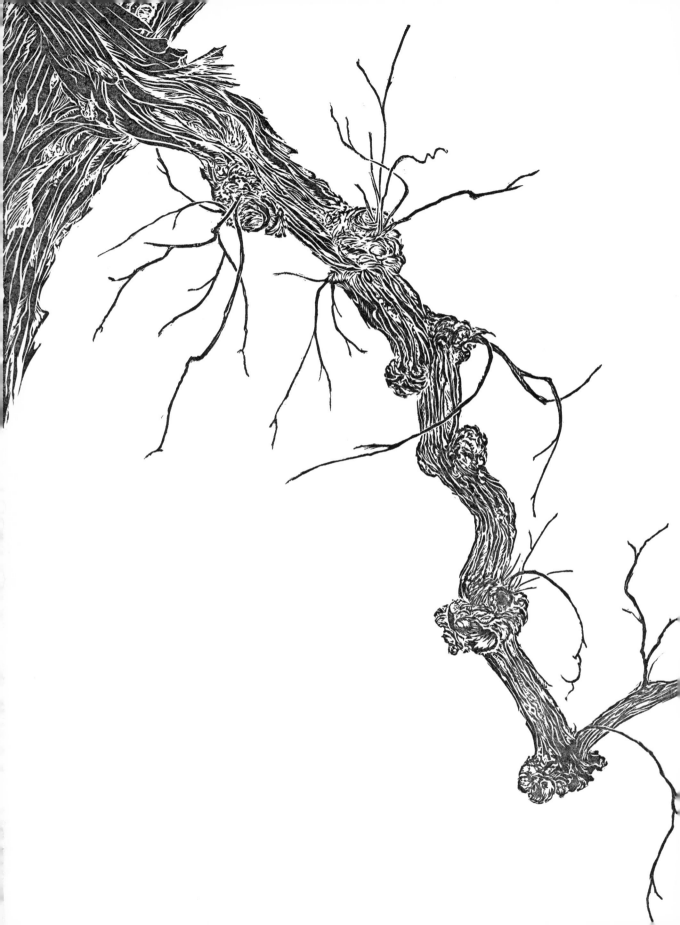

The ceaseless flow of the tides - -
            little sanderlings at the water's edge -
    sunrises - - and stars —
        wild geese in the airways - -
            red-wings singing of springtime -
                flowers blossoming in the open fields - - -

        - - from origin to termination -   - -
                the whole universe is involved with time . . . . . .

    The sempiternal rhythm
                that synchronizes all rhythms . . . . .

The entire sequential order
                speaks through the language of time —
    through time - -
        the immeasurable periods of evolution -
            the succession of the cycles - -
                the infallibility of balance - - -
                and the process of symmetrization - -
                                    are verified . . . .

Time — witness to infinite changes - - -
            as constant development
                shapes the earth and everything upon it . . . . .

Slow transformation that created mountains and valleys —
                        oceans and running brooks -
        continues to make new peaks - - and new lows -
                as each life changes with it . . . . .

Visible and impalpable movements - -
- - - the inevitable changes of age -
and a multitude of minute modifications
that will never cease . . . . .

The insects of ages gone by
ever so slowly became the insects of today —
and so with the trees - the birds - - and man . . . .

Imperceptible transformation - - - -
- and life - - not adapting to change - - -
but in natural order
changes with change . . . . .

Man sees and responds to alteration in the environment —
and - in a vague way - in life around him - - -
he cannot conceive of himself interlocked
in this continual miracle . . . . . .

He rejects far reaching predictions -
unaware that as the future
becomes the present - -
man will be a natural part of it . . . . .

As the time lag between man's actions - -
and the consequences of his acts is shortening - - -
he is beginning to comprehend
the magnitude of each decision . . . . . .

Realizing that his attempts to mutilate time
to suit his own desires —
to harness the energy of the earth
to make time —
his impulse for speed in every aspect of his life — —
has created a hollow man . . . . .

To man's two great assets - -
    discovery and invention - -
        must be added evaluation —
            that he may coordinate his inventions
                        with the natural milieu . . . . . .

To a bird on the wing
                time is now - - - -
    - to man
            it is all his yesterdays - -
                - the tomorrows he hopes to have -
                    and - the present he so often neglects . . . .

He need not allow time to be his master - - -
                        but a natural ally in his fulfillment . . .
    It is not necessary that he be totally enslaved
                            by appointed hours —
        but that he allow some moments when
                        imagination and creativeness
            are free to explore the islands of serenity
                            that surround him . . . . .

        Moments when he will find himself
                in complete communion with
                    the rhythms of the universe - - -
                        - attuned to the timelessness of time . . . .

Time in unlimited abundance —
        - - always on the side of nature -
            moves inexorably on - through all the changes - - -
                - rhythm - - harmony and mystery - - -
                        - - - remain . . . .

NYMPH — AFTER MANY MONTHS IN A POND - -
climbs to the bank - - or clings to a reed -
— its armor splits - - and a colorful dragonfly
darts into the sunshine . . . .

As natural a phenomenon as man's slow evolutionary climb . . . . . .
The process of cumulative change
that transforms his thinking - - -
enables him to create great new concepts - -
as he explores a fresh sense of wonder —
and finds in nature - - freedom within boundaries -
unity and order in knowledge . . .

He will not turn back - - -
for the primary rule of the universe
is to reach out to new directions —
- - - and man is no exception - -
He cannot escape the basic laws of nature . . . . . .

From the time the ancient bird
developed the power of flight
it perfected its ability to fly - -
never to return to the sea again
- as a reptile - -
— and - the dragonfly will not turn back
to its life as a nymph . . . . . .

As the human mind —

    evolving through the ages - -

        analyzes the obvious

            it will accept the harmonious order

                    to which man belongs - - -

            with all its inter-relationships - -

                - its inter-dependencies —

                    and - its freedom of choices . . . . .

Man - cognizing that

        his keen powers of observation -

            his deep understandings - -

                and his vast knowledge - - -

            will help him discover what nature is doing —

                    occasionally how - - - but never why - - - -

        — nature always speaks in mysterious enigmas —

    will pursue the art of sensing

                the unity that lies beyond apparent differences . . . . . .

Greater by far than his knowledge of facts -

        - which is the wellspring of every creative mind - -

    is his search for attunement between knowledge and action . . . .

Then he will dedicate his body - - mind —

                    and his spirit

                to the highest development of man's being . . . .

    Abandon his age of destruction and waste - -

                seek quality rather than excessive quantities . . .

He will build in unity with his natural allies - -
    the winds - the rains - and the sun - - -
        as primary sources of heat - light - - and productivity —
            rather than to protect himself against these elements . . . .
He will work diligently
    toward a whole new concept of transportation - - -
        knowing that however ingenious the development
                        of the automobile was - - -
            it must yield to something infinitely greater
                        beyond . . . .
man will accept the axiom of nature - -
        blending the old with the new - - -
            use no more than can be produced - - - -
                and find that in its entity - - no waste exists . . . . .
    He will no longer pounce on each new idea
            with such enthusiasm that all wisdom is lost - -
                with the alacrity that makes
                        today's discovery
                            obsolete by tomorrow's dawn . . . .
As the dragonfly
            darted into new life in the sunshine - - - - -
        man will find ultimate harmony
                    in intimate things - - -
            and rejoice in the knowledge
                        that he is an intrinsic part of it all . . . . . .

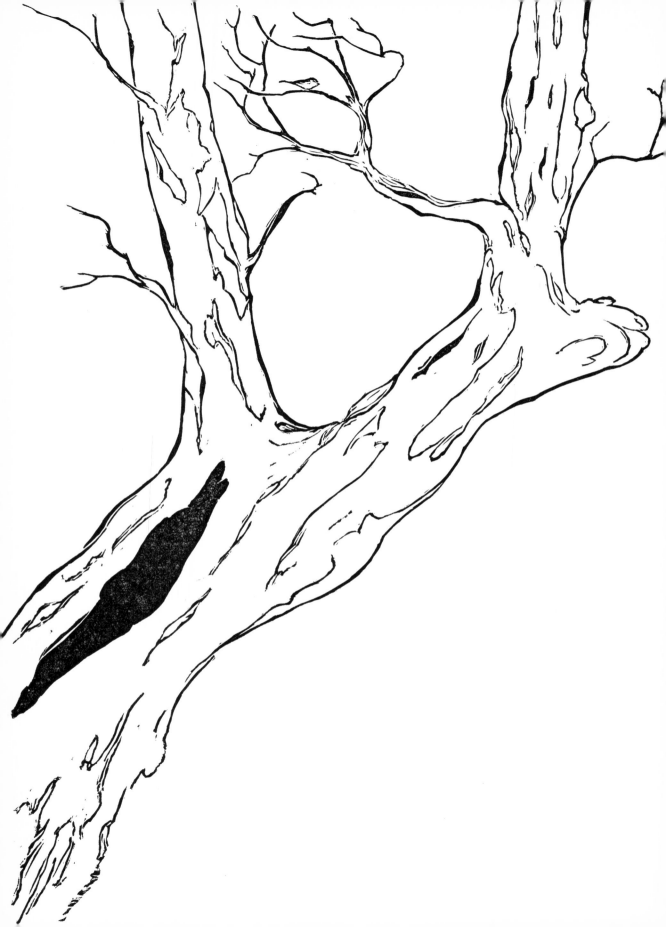

OW — MAN IS EMERGING FROM THE TIGHT COCOON
of specialists - - -
- THE LAWYERS - - THE MILITARY - - -
SCIENTISTS - - AND ECONOMISTS —
WHO ABETTED HIM TO ASSUME THAT ALL PROBLEMS
COULD BE SOLVED BY TECHNICAL KNOWLEDGE ALONE . . . . .
A COCOON THAT STIFLED MAN'S AVIDITY
TO SEARCH FOR FACTS TO MAKE DECISIONS
WITH HIS OWN KNOWLEDGE AND MIND . . . .
HE IS SLOWLY COMING TO THE REALIZATION
THAT PROBLEMS CREATED BY THIS ENTOMBMENT
ARE ENORMOUSLY GREATER THAN THE PROTECTION IT OFFERS . . .
PERHAPS IT WAS A PHASE MAN HAD TO EXPERIENCE - -
AS A CATERPILLAR MUST REMAIN IN ITS COCOON
BEFORE BECOMING A BUTTERFLY . . . . . .
EMERGING - HE WILL ENTER AN ERA OF PERSONAL INGENUITY AND WISDOM -
- - ABANDON HIS DREAM OF AUTOMATIC SECURITY - - -
HE WILL USE THE REASONING OF HIS OWN MIND
BASED UPON THE RESEARCH OF CENTURIES GONE BY - -
AND FIND THAT THE FOUNTAIN-HEAD OF FAITH IS KNOWLEDGE . . .
WITH NEW PERSPECTIVE HE WILL SEE
THE INDEPENDENCE WITHIN DEPENDENCY
OF ALL LIFE UPON THIS EARTH - - -
AND UNDERSTAND THE GREAT INTER-INVOLVEMENT
AND AT ONCE THE INDIVIDUALISM OF IT . . . . .
HE WILL BEGIN TO COMPREHEND THAT MAN CANNOT
LIVE A LIFE UNTO HIMSELF — CREATING THINGS FOR MAN ALONE - -
THAT SHORTAGES ARE CAUSED BY MAN'S EXCESSIVE DESIRES - - -
HIS WANTON WASTES - - - - AND CARELESSNESS . . . .
- - - NOW THAT THE COCOON IS BROKEN - - - -
HE WILL BE FREE TO DEVELOP A LUCID AND PENETRATING MIND
WITH A PASSION FOR KNOWLEDGE - -
AND VISION THAT SEES BEYOND THE SEGMENTATION OF THINGS - -
AND BEHOLDS THE COSMOS . . .

Man staked his fate
        on his calculations -
                equations - -
                        his computers - - -
                and his massive movers - - -
        as he conquered each mechanical
                challenge that faced him . . . .
The machine he had been building
        screw by screw - -
                gear by gear - - -
        since the beginning of the wheel
                became his greatest credit
                and - aroused his
                        gravest anxieties . . . .

The computerizing of all things into
        categories with external controls -
                developed a man lost in a maze
                of numbers - - an indifferent man
        — indifferent to the world of nature - -
                - - indifferent to other human beings
                - - - indifferent to himself . . . . . .

A man lost in loneliness - - -
        without the joy of creative
                individualism . . . . .

THE MACHINE SHOULD HAVE BEEN AN EXTENSION
                of THE NATURAL WAYS OF THE UNIVERSE - - -
                                - - NOT A THING UNTO ITSELF . . . . .
BUT MAN FORGOT - - -
    HE BECAME ENGROSSED WITH BUILDING HIS EUPHORIA —
            THROUGH THE FULFILLMENT OF HIS OWN DESIRES - -
                    - AND THE TOTAL MASTERY OF NATURE - - -
        ONE IN WHICH ALL MAN'S ACTIONS WOULD BECOME
                                AUTOMATIC AND EFFORTLESS . . . .
HE WAS UNWITTINGLY CREATING AN EMPTY MAN
                        DEVOID OF THE INCENTIVES
                                THAT STIMULATE THOUGHT . . .
BUT CHANGE WILL COME - - - - -
                s l o w l y — —
                    AS SLOWLY AS ALL UNIVERSAL EVOLUTION - -
                                - - - AND JUST AS INFALLIBLE . . . . .
ON THE HORIZON A DAY IS DAWNING
    WHEN MAN WILL TAKE THE MAGNIFICENT ACHIEVEMENTS
                            OF SCIENCE AND TECHNOLOGY -
        AND FUSE THEM WITH THE ART OF SENSING THE
                            WHOLENESS OF THE UNIVERSE . . . . .
A DAY WHEN HUMAN ENERGY WILL NOT BE WASTED
                    ON HOSTILITIES TOWARD NATURE - OR MAN - - -
    - WHEN THE RISING TIDE OF INDIVIDUALISM
                        - WITHIN THE UNITY OF ONE UNIVERSE -
        WILL INITIATE THE PERCEPTION OF A SINGLE WHOLE —
            TO WHICH ALL ENERGY IS DIRECTED - -
                    AND - FROM WHICH ALL ENERGY IS DERIVED . . . . .
A WHOLE DEPENDENT UPON
        EACH INDIVIDUAL PART RESPONDING FULLY TO ITS OWN NEEDS - - -
                    TO ACHIEVE CONTINUANCE . . . .

Creator God Breathes

BETWEEN THE EARTH AND THE STARS —

- - - - THE AIR - - -

invisible and formless — ever in motion
inextricably linked to everything on earth . . . .

In the amplitude of air
clouds - rainbows - - and snowflakes form —
thunder - lightning - and great storms rage —
- - - and calm and beauty interplay . . . . .

Clouds — perpetually new — ascending to lofty heights
clouds - upon clouds - - upon clouds - - -
catching the rays of the sun and reflecting them back and forth
until the cloud itself is an immense luminous movement . . .

— then it resolves itself
and disappears into the clear blue sky
— to begin anew . . .

A feeling of freedom and ecstasy stirs the soul . . . .

Feathery clouds - - invisible needles of ice
stretch in long lines across far horizons
or a heavy unbroken blanket shuts out the sun
— and the day seems dark —
then - it too - moves on - - dissolving into air . . . . . .

In the darkness of night — the air glows
and a multitude of shapes continuously shifting reach toward the zenith
curtains of glistening whites - greens - - and reds
flashing and flickering in the sky
as tiny solar missiles electrify the polar air . . . .

Moments of splendor — and awe . . . .

Flowing easily in all directions
        the air shelters the earth and all the life upon it
                        from the blazing sun . . .

As long as there is air - there will be
        sound - color - - and fragrance
            hawks - grasses - bees —
                and gentle breezes in the trees . . .

Since earth and time began —
        the air has been its own regulator
            maintaining its own delicate balance - - -

    — true to the dominant miracle
                    of the universe
            sustaining self
                with benevolence to all . . . . .

Between the earth and the stars - -
        the air - *male - female*

                and so the stars twinkle . . . . . .

*and we breathe this air
this very air in Jesus*

HE COSMOS ENDURES - - -

THE UNCHANGING RHYTHMS OF THE UNIVERSE
ARE ETERNAL - - -

AND — life perpetuates life . . . .

THE PRESENT
ORIGINATED IN THE PAST - - -
AND GENERATES THE FUTURE . . . .

Loveliness -
HARMONY - -
AND WONDER
ARE TIMELESS . . . .

$\mathcal{L}$ive without thinking about living - -
　　　　　believe without seeking proof - - -
Feel a sense of kinship
　　　　　with every living thing —
In moments of solitude
　　　　　hear all of nature singing - -
And - dream of the wonderment and beauty
　　　　　of the enduring cosmos . . . .